Being Respectful

Joanna Ponto

 Enslow Publishing
101 W. 23rd Street
Suite 240
New York, NY 10011
USA
enslow.com

Published in 2016 by Enslow Publishing, LLC.
101 W. 23rd Street, Suite 240, New York, NY 10011

Library of Congress Cataloging-in-Publication Data
Ponto, Joanna, author.
 Being respectful / Joanna Ponto.
     pages cm. — (All about character)
 Summary: "Provides character education through different scenarios that demonstrate children being respectful"— Provided by publisher.
 Audience: Ages 4-6
 Audience: K to grade 3
 Includes bibliographical references and index.
 ISBN 978-0-7660-7099-8 (library binding)
 ISBN 978-0-7660-7097-4 (pbk.)
 ISBN 978-0-7660-7098-1 (6-pack)
 1. Respect for persons—Juvenile literature. 2. Respect—Juvenile literature. 3. Conduct of life—Juvenile literature. I. Title.
 BJ1533.R42P66 2016
 179.9—dc23
                    2015000155

Printed in the United States of America

To Our Readers: We have done our best to make sure all Web sites in this book were active and appropriate when we went to press. However, the author and the publisher have no control over and assume no liability for the material available on those Web sites or on any Web sites they may link to. Any comments or suggestions can be sent by e-mail to customerservice@enslow.com.

Photo Credits: Alex011973/Shutterstock.com, p. 20; Andersen Ross/Blend Images/Getty Images, pp. 3 (center), 6; Blend Images/Shutterstock.com, pp. 3 (left), 14; Diego Cervo/Shutterstock.com, pp. 3 (right), 4–5; Fuse/Thinkstock, p. 8; JGI/Jamie Grill/Blend Images/Getty Images, p. 18; Jupiterimages/Photos.com/Thinkstock, p. 10; Jupiterimages/Stockbyte/Thinkstock, p. 16; Monkey Business Images/Shutterstock.com, p. 12; Volodymyr Baleha/Shutterstock.com, p. 1; wavebreakmedia/Shutterstock.com, p. 22.

Cover Credit: Monkey Business Images/Shutterstock.com (boy raising hand).

Contents

Words to Know

listen

manners

respectful

A person who is respectful treats everyone fairly. He or she uses good manners. A person who is respectful accepts differences in people.

Luna walked up to the library door. A man with a hurt leg was trying to open the door. Luna held the door open for him. Luna is respectful.

Tracy and Joey were at the movies. Joey wanted to tell Tracy something. Joey waited until the movie was over to talk so he would not bother anybody. Joey is respectful.

Trang was playing football in her backyard. The football went into her neighbor's yard by mistake. Trang asked her neighbor if it was okay to get her ball back. Trang is respectful.

Theo had a question in class. Theo raised his hand. He waited until his teacher called on him before he asked his question. Theo is respectful.

Deedra likes to talk to her friends before school starts. When the bell rings, Deedra stops talking and sits down at her desk. She is ready to listen. Deedra is respectful.

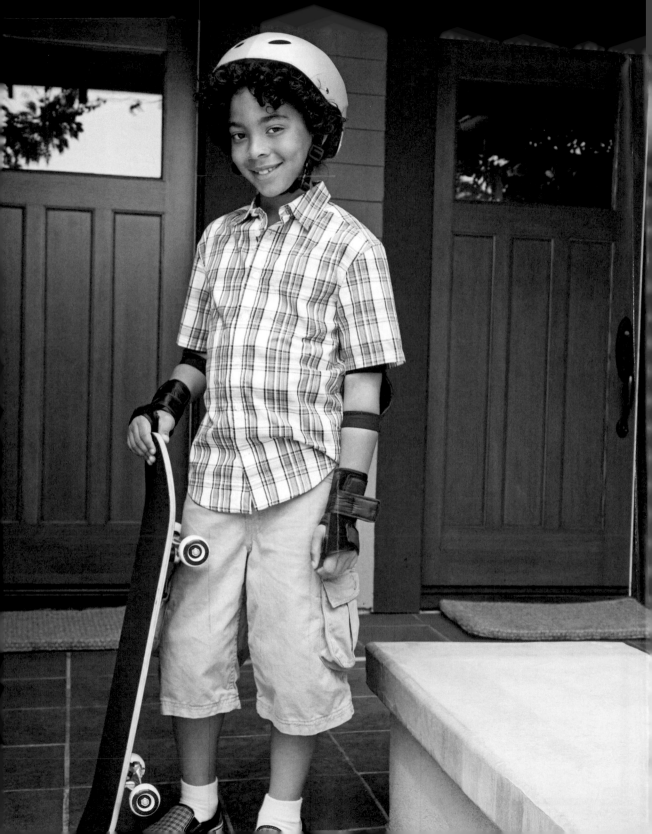

Pedro's brother got a new skateboard. Pedro wanted to ride it. He asked his brother first. His brother said yes. Pedro is respectful.

Holly's mother told her to clean her room. Holly stopped what she was doing. She put away all her toys and made her bed. Holly is respectful.

Maggie wanted to watch TV. Her sister had to study for a test. Maggie went into another room to watch TV. Maggie is respectful.

Peter wanted to show his father a game on the computer. His father was working. Peter waited until his father was finished and then showed him. Peter is respectful.

Read More

Higgins, Melissa. *I Am Respectful*. North Mankato, Minn.: Capstone Press, 2014.

Yankee, Kris, and Marian Nelson. *Are You Respectful Today?* Northville, Mich.: Ferne Press, 2014.

Web Sites

Kids' Health: Respect—A Way of Life
cyh.com/SubDefault.aspx?p=255

Talking With Trees: Respect Quotes
talkingtreebooks.com/quotes_for_kids.html#Respect

Index

Guided Reading Level: C
Guided Reading Leveling System is based on the guidelines recommended by Fountas and Pinnell.

Word Count: 275